The Other Side Of The Rainbow

Charlie Alex

The Other Side Of The Rainbow © 2022
Charlie Alex

All rights reserved.

Charlie Alex asserts the moral right to be identified as author of this work.

Presentation by *BookLeaf Publishing*

Web: www.bookleafpub.com

E-mail: info@bookleafpub.com

ISBN: 9789357614221

First edition 2022

Sink or swim

I'm drowning
In an ocean of regrets

I'm praying
That I never forget

I'm begging
Hoping you can hear me

I'm crying
Wishing you could see

I'm remorseful
Not taking advantage of each day

I feel a fool
For all the things that I didn't say

I'm ruminating
The unspoken words go round in my head

I'm mourning
Thinking of all the things I should have said

I'm frustrated
That I never made those calls

I'm hopeful
That God will cherish your soul

Yet still
I drown in this ocean
This sea of regret

Waiting til we meet again
But until then
These memories I'll never forget

MRN #63305

I am just a number
Just a burden to the system
Just another person
Just another victim

They say it gets better
I ask them "when?"
Because I've been going round in circles
And it seems to never end

Because as the sun goes down
At the end of the day
It'll still rise again tomorrow
Regardless of whether or not I stay

And the moon will still come out
And the birds will keeping singing
I just won't be around to see it
But the world will keep spinning

Who knows what comes next
No one can be sure
But if this is as good as life gets
I don't want to be here anymore

Prisoner Of War

I am a prisoner of my own mind
Trapped by these thoughts
There's a war in my head
And I've lost each battle I've fought

I am facing the judge
With a jury of demons
Sentenced to life
Without a good reason

Lock me up
Let me rot in this cell
I can't run away
For I can't escape myself

Broken Bottles

I am drowning
As you watch from the shore
I am suffocating
Anchored down to the floor

It's not me doing it
It had been you from the start
With one sip of your poison
My whole world is torn apart

The eyes all stare
Judging from the distance
Watching me suffer
While offering no assistance

The shame is overwhelming
And the guilt causes a physical ache
To drown in your poison
Was my biggest mistake

Stolen Flowers

I miss the days
When we would wake up early
Just to put on the tv
And watch our favourite shows

I miss the afternoons
When we would come home from school
And tell our parents proudly
All about what we did that day

I miss the nights
When we couldn't sleep from excitement
Eagerly awaiting
For the sun to rise the next morning

But more than all
I miss those precious moments
Before you wrongfully stole
What was so clearly mine

Because if I'm being honest
What I miss more than anything
Is the days when I would wake up
And to not wish I didn't wake up at all

Silent Screams

These thoughts don't stop
There's not a moments rest

I want to switch my brain off
I don't want to feel such a mess

These thoughts go round
Like a song on constant replay

So I lie on the ground
Curled in a ball to make it all go away

These thoughts don't shut up
They just keep getting louder

I'm ready to give up
But it just gives them more power

These thoughts don't stop
There's not a moments rest

As I tie the knot
I will no longer be obsessed

Flowers For The Broken Hearted

I am broken
Shattered into pieces
Like a glass vase
Scattered
On the ground all over

And as I try to clean up
The shard fragments
Of the mess I have made
I wonder to myself
If I can ever truly recover

For this damage
Is much too severe
And this hurt
Is a wound
That never closes

And I know
Deep down
That if it weren't for you
My vase
Would still be filled with roses

Genesis 2:21

Even Adam and Eve
Were tricked by the serpent
So mesmerised by the sin
There was no care for consequence

You lure me in
With your addictive taste
The toxicity you bleed
Pulls me toward my fate

And the venom you bring forth
Makes my lips burn
The euphoria is an enticement
To succumb to the urge

So here's to you
Because I let you win
After all
I am a sucker for your poison

Elephants Memory

I remember how I felt afterwards
So disgusting and dirty
I knew it didn't matter how much I was bathe
I could never get rid of your touch

I remember the moments before hand
How I ignored the butterflies in my stomach
I walked into the unknown shaking
Consumed by the thrill rush

I remember the moment I saw your face
And the feeling of my stomach drop
Not knowing what would happen next
And being scared to find out

I remember wanting it to be over
Yet pretending otherwise
I remember hating myself afterwards
Wondering how foolish could I be

I remember the nights I lie in bed
Trying to erase the memory from my mind
I remember the hesitation to trust
And the paranoid thoughts that follow

I remember
But I wish I didn't

Jewellery Thief

I miss you
I miss the warmth of your hug
I miss the scent of your perfume

I miss you
I miss watching you curl your hair
I miss watching you fiddle with your rings

I miss you
I miss the sigh of relief I'd feel when I'd see
your face
I miss the feeling of my heart skip a beat as we'd
pull into your driveway

I miss you
I miss hearing you laugh when you didn't
understand the joke
I miss hearing you sing when you didn't know
the lyrics

I miss you
I miss the days I'd wake up eager to see you
I miss the sleepless nights too excited to for the
next day

But if I'm being honest
What I miss the most
Is the times when I went to bed
Where I knew you'd be there the next morning

What I miss more than anything
Is the nights I'd go to bed
And I didn't wish that the next day I wouldn't
wake up
Because I knew I didn't have you to wake up to

Twenty Seven Bottles Of Beer

Rolling the dice with death
Hoping to forget
Seeing how far I can push it
Til I drown in my regrets

This emptiness physically hurts
Yet inside I feel so numb
Twenty seven drinks down
Who have I become

I don't want to remember
I want to cease to exist
It's only getting harder
To cross each line off my bucket list

Please save me I'm drowning
In an ocean of regret
Yet another bottle I'm downing
Finally I can forget

What Doesn't Kill You

They say what doesn't kill you
Only makes you stronger

But in reality

What doesn't kill me
Leaves me with open wounds

What doesn't kill me
Leaves me with a broken heart

What doesn't kill me
Leaves me with emotional damage

What doesn't kill me
Makes me wish it did

B.T. 13

Because of you
Every person I see
Never feels deserving of trust

But you never meant to hurt me
Even in the moments that hurt the most
None of it was done intentionally

Because that's what you told me
Even looked me dead in the eyes
Nodding as you assured me

But it was intentional
Eventually it ended in flames
No sooner to be forgotten about

Blatantly taken advantage of
Evidence ignored
Never again to be discussed

But
Even if
No one else remembers

I do, Ben.

Unanswered Questions

How could you hit
A child so small
And helpless
While seeing the fear in their eyes

How could you tell them
That they are a burden
How could you say
You hope she dies

How could you hurt
A child you willingly brought into this world
When you claimed you would give
Them nothing but care

How could you
How
I want to know what I did wrong
I want to know what I did to deserve such
despair

Stolen Hopes, Broken Dreams

I made it very clear
There was no room
For misinterpretation

It seems you understood
You just didn't care
Couldn't resist the temptation

But like the criminal you are
You stole what wasn't yours
Something that I can't replace

And the part that bothers me the most
Strangely enough
Is that you were never mine in the first place

It Was My Fault

It was my fault
I didn't say no enough

It was my fault
I was drunk

It was my fault
I should have stayed somewhere else

It was my fault
I should have just left straight away

It was my fault
I didn't see the red flags

It was my fault
I shouldn't have put myself in danger

It was my fault
It always is

Right, mum?

Moby Dick

How can I feel sad
When I don't truly know the truth?
How can I mourn
When I don't even know what I've lost?

How can I grieve
Or be angry or annoyed?
How can I feel I've been stolen from
When I never knew the cost?

How do I stop myself
From feeling such a fraud?
How do I stop
These feelings of guilt and defeat?

Part of me knows
But doesn't want to admit.
But deep down I know
You are nothing but a thief.

Flip A Coin

You were the first
The first of many if I'm honest
But it was you
Who first broke my heart

You lured me in
With your lies and devious ways
You had me a fool
From the very start

And like a cut from a knife
This wound goes deep
And your empty threats
Carry a heavy burden

Even after all this time
I still resent you
But it'll be over my dead body
That you ever hurt me again

Unheard Words

It seems that the silence
Speaks louder than words
And the unspoken agreement
Is crystal clear

Perhaps you forgot
I did tell you before
That I didn't really want to
Maybe you didn't hear

But I did agree after all
In fact
I was the one
Who suggested it

Although I felt that
It was expected of me
I'm still the only one
That regrets it

Coincidences Aren't Always Coincidental

It's just a coincidence
Maybe I wasn't screaming in a bad way

It's just a coincidence
You promised you'd wear a condom anyway

It's just a coincidence
When I went to the toilet and saw the blood all
over my hands

It's just a coincidence
Using my drunkenness to ask for money to your
advance

It's just a coincidence
That I was blackout drunk and you hadn't been
drinking

It's just a coincidence
That you used me while drunk, and I wasn't
clearly thinking

It's just a coincidence
These bruises could have happened in a drunken
fall

It wasn't a coincidence
It wasn't a coincidence at all

Betty 1934

The words left unspoken,
Will always be my biggest regret.
I can't tell you how I feel,
After you've already left.

And to know that you'll never know,
Just how much I truly cared for you,
Causes an ache deep in my soul,
And breaks my heart in two.

And I wish I knew it before,
That at the end of the day,
I'll forever regret,
The words I didn't say.